The Inside Guide

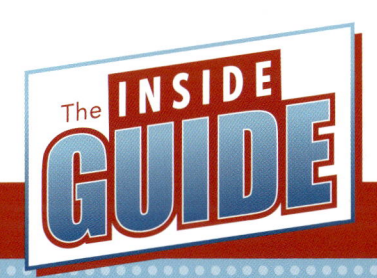

DOCUMENTS OF DEMOCRACY

The Magna Carta

By Sadie Silva

Cavendish Square

New York

Published in 2022 by Cavendish Square Publishing, LLC
29 East 21st Street, New York, NY 10010

Copyright © 2022 by Cavendish Square Publishing, LLC

First Edition

No part of this publication may be reproduced, stored in a retrieval system, or transmitted in any form or by any means—electronic, mechanical, photocopying, recording, or otherwise—without the prior permission of the copyright owner. Request for permission should be addressed to Permissions, Cavendish Square Publishing, 29 East 21st Street, New York, NY 10010. Tel (877) 980-4450; fax (877) 980-4454.

Website: cavendishsq.com

This publication represents the opinions and views of the author based on his or her personal experience, knowledge, and research. The information in this book serves as a general guide only. The author and publisher have used their best efforts in preparing this book and disclaim liability rising directly or indirectly from the use and application of this book.

All websites were available and accurate when this book was sent to press.

Portions of this work were originally authored by Janey Levy and published as *The Magna Carta (Documents That Shaped America)*. All new material this edition authored by Sadie Silva.

Library of Congress Cataloging-in-Publication Data

Names: Silva, Sadie, author.
Title: The Magna Carta / Sadie Silva.
Description: New York : Cavendish Square Publishing, [2022] | Series: The inside guide: documents of democracy | Includes index.
Identifiers: LCCN 2020045602 | ISBN 9781502660442 (library binding) | ISBN 9781502660428 (paperback) | ISBN 9781502660435 (set) | ISBN 9781502660459 (ebook)
Subjects: LCSH: Magna Carta–Juvenile literature. | Magna Carta–Influence–Juvenile literature.
Classification: LCC JN147 .S45 2022 | DDC 323.44–dc23
LC record available at https://lccn.loc.gov/2020045602

Editor: Caitie McAneney
Copyeditor: Jill Keppeler
Designer: Jessica Nevins

The photographs in this book are used by permission and through the courtesy of: Cover photos.com/Getty Images; pp. 4, 6, 16, 27 Universal History Archive/Universal Images Group via Getty Images; p. 7 PHAS/Universal Images Group via Getty Images; p. 8 Historica Graphica Collection/Heritage Images/Getty Images; pp. 9, 18, 20 (top) The Print Collector/Getty Images; pp. 10, 29 (top) © Historical Picture Archive/CORBIS/Corbis via Getty Images; p. 12 Henry Guttmann Collection/Hulton Archive/Getty Images; p. 13 Museum of London/Heritage Images/Getty Images; p. 14 Archive Photos/Getty Images; p. 19 Photo 12/Universal Images Group via Getty Images; p. 20 (bottom) Parliament of England/Wikimedia Commons/File:Petition of Right.jpg; p. 22 Kirkikis/iStock Editorial/Getty Images Plus/Getty Images; pp. 23, 25, 29 (bottom) Hulton Archive/Getty Images; p. 24 Stock Montage/Stock Montage/Getty Images; p. 26 (top) Universal History Archive/Getty Images; p. 26 (bottom) Fotosearch/Getty Images.

Some of the images in this book illustrate individuals who are models. The depictions do not imply actual situations or events.

CPSIA compliance information: Batch #CW22CSQ: For further information contact Cavendish Square Publishing LLC, New York, New York, at 1-877-980-4450.

Printed in the United States of America

Find us on

CONTENTS

Chapter One: 5
   Feudal Feuds

Chapter Two: 11
   The Great Charter

Chapter Three: 17
   A Seed of Democracy

Chapter Four: 23
   Inspiring a New Nation

How the Magna Carta Inspired
Documents of Democracy 28

Think About It! 29

Glossary 30

Find Out More 31

Index 32

King Henry II (1133–1189) was the father of Richard I and John Lackland. Like kings before him, he had absolute power over his subjects.

FEUDAL FEUDS

Chapter One

Today, there are many documents of **democracy** that influence our ideas about our rights and liberties as citizens. However, the founding documents of the United States have their roots in an ancient, or very old, document called the Magna Carta. The Magna Carta, passed in 1215, influenced new democracies around the world.

Society Under Feudalism

Feudalism was the main social, military, and political system in medieval Europe between the 9th and 14th centuries. In feudal England, the king owned all the land. He granted some nobles, or barons, plots of land called fiefs. At the bottom of society were peasants, who lived on a noble's fief and farmed it for him. The nobles and peasants were all vassals, or subjects, of the king.

The king oversaw his court, which was made up of his nobles. As a group, the nobles made decisions to resolve any quarrels, or disagreements, between

Fast Fact

In return for his fief, a noble pledged his loyalty and service to the king. When the king went to war, a noble had to provide money or manpower as aid.

themselves. Nobles involved in quarrels were required to obey a summons, or an order to appear in court. If a noble refused to appear or disobeyed the court's decision, the king could take back his fief. The king had absolute power, which sometimes led to **tyranny**.

King John, the Tyrant

King John of England (ca. 1166–1216) was seen largely as an irresponsible, power-hungry tyrant. As the youngest son of King Henry II, John even tried to steal the throne from his older brother, Richard I (also known as Richard the Lionheart). However, after Richard's death, John became king in 1199.

Soon after taking the throne, King John went to war with France. By 1206, John had lost England's territories in France. He waged war for 10 years, trying unsuccessfully to regain those lands. Taxes rose steeply to finance the war, angering the nobles. Those who didn't provide knights had to pay three times the normal fee. Those who didn't pay were fined. John also heavily taxed the barons' land and household possessions.

King John, also known as John Lackland, was an unpopular king, known for his selfishness and irresponsible leadership.

Fast Fact
John was **banished** from England in 1194 for trying to steal Richard's throne while he was away at war. They later **reconciled**, or made up.

Richard the Lionheart was unlike his brother John. He was a popular king who went to war for his country and Christian faith in the Third Crusade (1189–1192).

THE ARTICLES OF THE BARONS

The Articles of the Barons document was presented to King John on June 10, 1215, at Runnymede, a meadow along the River Thames. The document consisted of 48 articles, which were demands by the barons. The demands ensured that barons could inherit land without having to pay fines. They ensured the king couldn't unfairly seize, or steal, land for debts. Sheriffs or royal officers also couldn't steal a free man's horses. These demands would make daily life fairer for barons and common people who lived under the king's power. King John had little choice but to agree to the Articles of the Barons. The document was edited, and five days later, was signed as the Magna Carta.

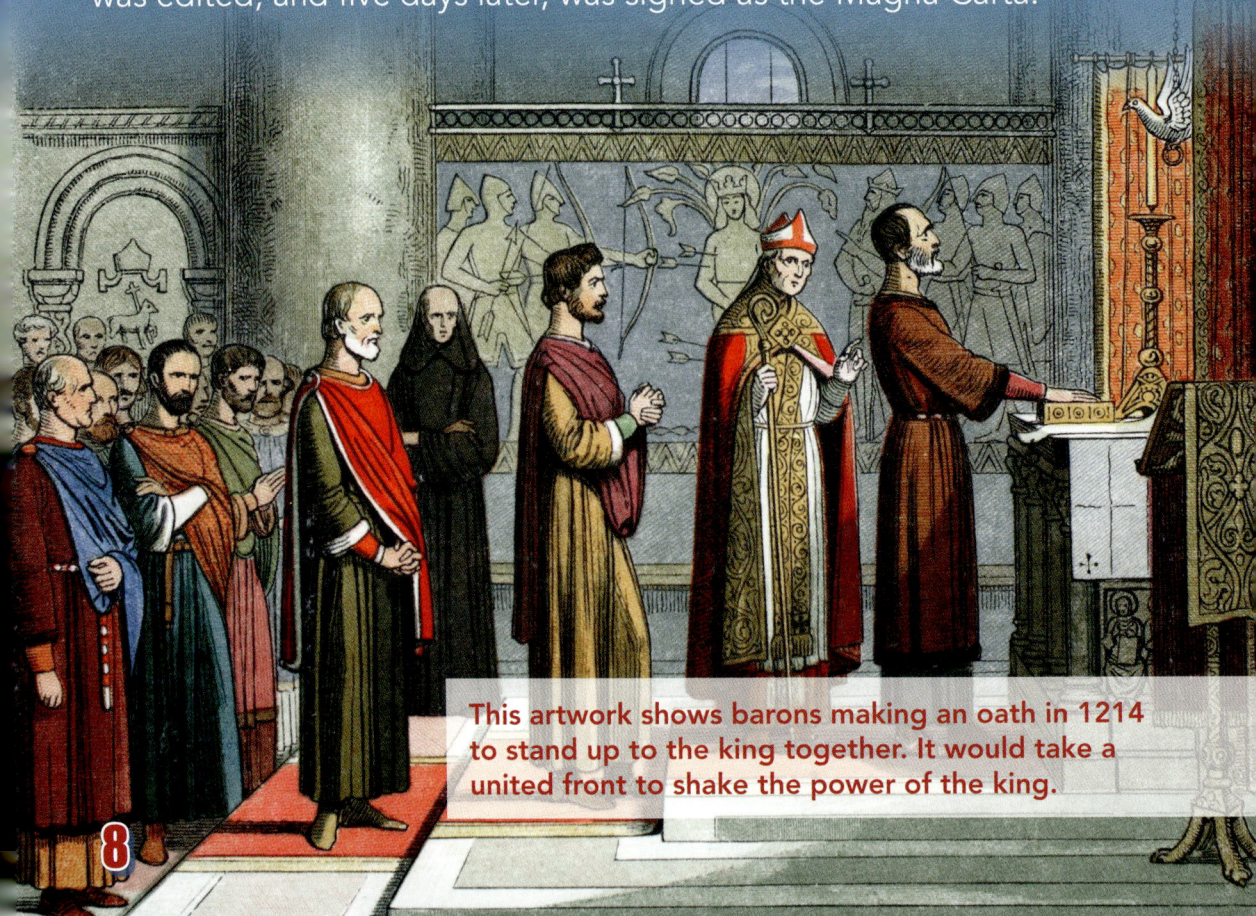

This artwork shows barons making an oath in 1214 to stand up to the king together. It would take a united front to shake the power of the king.

The barons and others were mistreated under John's rule. The king kept close watch over their land and income. He launched wars against barons he thought were plotting against him. By 1215, the barons had had enough. A civil war broke out in May 1215, and John faced a rebellion that could upend the kingdom. The barons presented their demands to John in the Articles of the Barons, which laid the basis for the Magna Carta.

Fast Fact

The legends of Robin Hood (the earliest of which date to around the 15th century) followed an outlaw who steals from the rich to give to the poor. King John was seen as an evil king in many of the legends—and in real life.

Robin Hood was an outlaw and hero in English legends. He was a champion of the common people, stealing from the rich to give to the poor.

King John's signing of the Magna Carta signaled a shift away from the absolute power of royals and toward democratic principles.

Chapter Two

THE GREAT CHARTER

Under great pressure, King John approved the Magna Carta, or "Great Charter," on June 15, 1215, and four days later, the agreement between the barons and the king was finalized. The Magna Carta consists of a preamble, or introduction, and 63 clauses, or articles. The clauses cover feudal laws of special concern to the barons, issues concerning towns and merchants, reforms of the law and of justice, and behavior of royal officials. The document ends by giving barons the right to take action against a king if he doesn't obey the charter. This was revolutionary—it meant that even the king was bound to the law.

Rights and Reforms

The Magna Carta was a major step toward ensuring rights and justice for subjects of the king. Clause 13 ensures that London and other cities and towns had certain rights and freedoms that couldn't be taken away by the king. Other clauses deal with subjects' rights and justice pertaining to heirs and widows.

Fast Fact
Earlier royal charters had been freely granted, while the barons forced the Great Charter on King John. Unlike the earlier charters, the Magna Carta was a challenge to the king's authority.

IMPROVING THE KINGDOM

The Magna Carta is known for laying out general principles of law. Many of these principles affected later documents of democracy and shaped future governments. However, some clauses in the Magna Carta deal with specific complaints over daily life and attempts to improve the kingdom. Clause 33, for example, promises to improve river navigation by removing weirs, or pens, placed in the waterways to catch fish. Clause 35 declares that there should be standard measures of wine, ale, and corn, and that there should be standard widths for cloth. Other clauses deal with regulation of the royal forests and taxes.

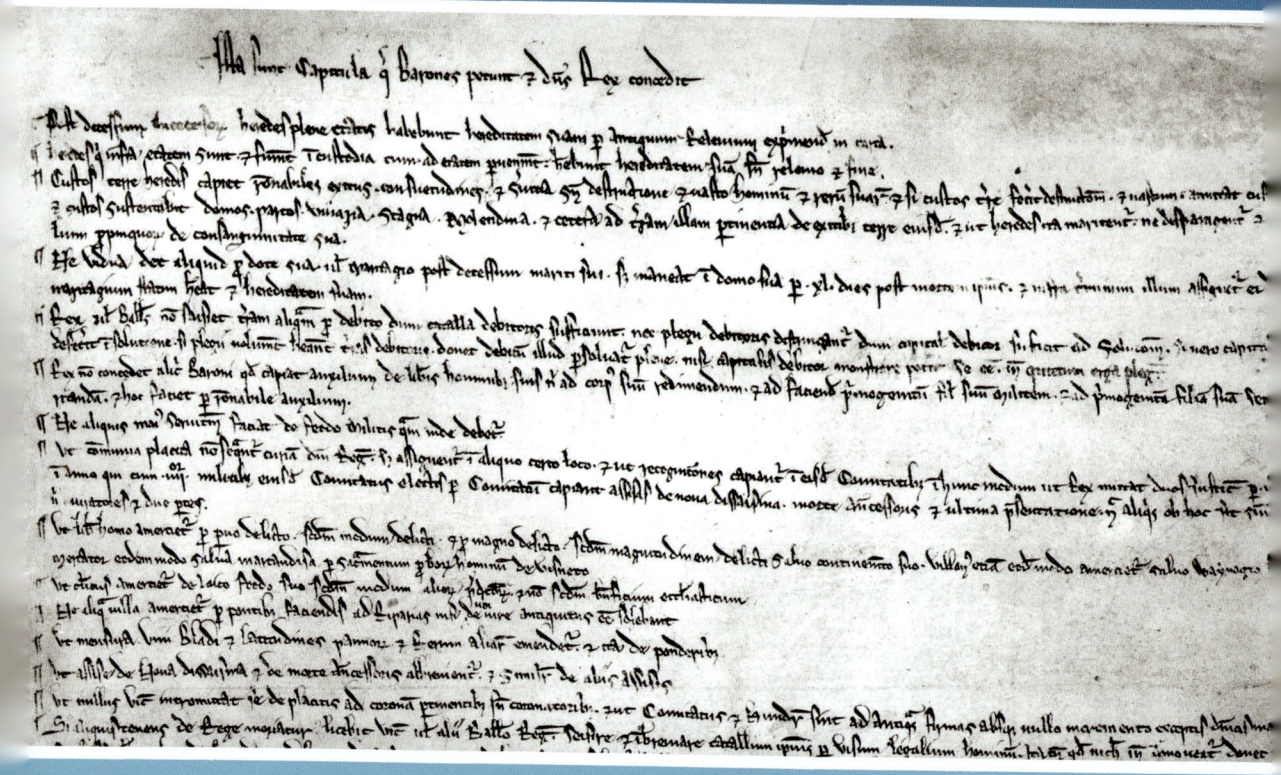

This image shows the text of the Magna Carta, which consists of 63 clauses.

The Charter of King John, shown here, was issued just a few weeks before the Magna Carta. It gave Londoners the right to choose their own mayor each year.

Clause 39 is one of the most well-known parts of the Magna Carta. It promises due process, which is the practice of applying laws fairly, and the right to judgment by one's peers. Clause 39 states, "No free man shall be seized or imprisoned, or stripped of his rights or possessions, or outlawed or exiled, or **deprived** of his standing in any other way, nor will we [the king] proceed with force against him, or send others to do so, except by the lawful judgment of his equals or by the law of the land."

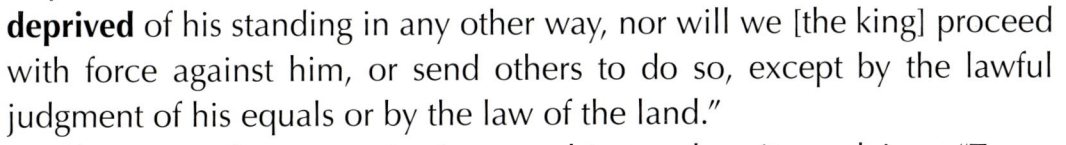

Clause 40 also grants justice to subjects when it proclaims, "To no one will we sell, to no one deny or delay right or justice." This simple line meant a great deal. It meant that no one could have their rights taken away or have to pay for them through bribes to the king. No one should have to wait for justice either, which ensured a prompt and fair trial for those accused of crimes.

Fast Fact

The first clause ensures the freedom of the English Church to elect its own leaders. This was included after a feud between the king and pope, or leader of the Catholic Church.

This artwork shows King John signing the Magna Carta under pressure from his subjects.

Limits on Royal Power

Before the Magna Carta was signed, the king could do what he wanted at the expense of his subjects, with no real limits on his power. The Magna Carta was revolutionary because it established that the king was not above the law.

According to clause 61, if the king or one of his officials broke any clauses in the Magna Carta, the barons could demand that the king make things right immediately. If the king took no action within 40 days, the barons could use force against him. They may "**assail** us [the king] in every way possible, with the support of the whole community of the land, by seizing our castles, lands, possessions, or anything else."

Other clauses place limits on royal power as well. They ensure that no royal official takes a free man's horses, carts, or wood. One clause establishes that "no official shall place a man on trial upon his [the official's] own unsupported statement, without producing **credible** witnesses to the truth of it." These clauses helped protect people from **corruption**.

Fast Fact

One of the most revolutionary clauses in the Magna Carta is the security clause (61). It gives barons the right to form a committee to take action against the king if he doesn't honor the charter.

King Henry III (1207–1272) wasn't an effective ruler, and conflicts with the barons continued throughout his reign.

A SEED OF DEMOCRACY

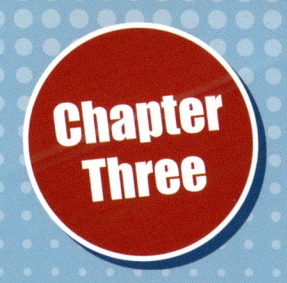

Chapter Three

The Magna Carta didn't end the **monarchy** in England. However, it planted a seed of democracy by giving free men rights and granting barons some power to check the king. The charter had its share of challenges from royalty, but also went on to inspire new thinkers, both in England and abroad.

Royal Pains

After the signing of the Magna Carta, copies were read throughout the kingdom. However, King John wasn't about to let this challenge to his authority stand. In 1216, he went back on the Magna Carta. The furious barons declared war. The short war ended upon John's death in October 1216. Then, his 9-year-old son, King Henry III, came into power. Henry's advisers, who made decisions for him because he was so young, made peace with the barons and reissued the Magna Carta.

The Magna Carta increased in importance, keeping peace between royals and nobles. Fearing another war, King Henry III's advisers reissued the Magna Carta again in 1217. In 1225, when Henry was old enough to assume his duties as king, he reissued the Magna Carta himself. He issued it again in 1264. In 1297, King Edward I even declared that all

King Edward I (1239–1307) amended, or changed, many laws, which shaped the English justice system for centuries.

judgments contrary to the Great Charter weren't binding. While some kings still abused their power, the Magna Carta had laid a foundation for limiting royals and giving rights to people.

Common Law

Centuries later, the Magna Carta inspired an English lawyer and judge named Edward Coke (pronounced "Cook"). Coke worked as a lawyer for the royal court under Queen Elizabeth I before becoming a judge in 1606. He believed in the power of common law. This body of law is based on **precedents** established over the centuries by judicial decisions rather than on **statutes** passed by **Parliament** or the king. Coke believed common law was superior to royal authority. He also believed rights and freedoms belonged to everyone, not just to nobles.

This artworks shows judges during Elizabeth I's reign, wearing official robes.

Edward Coke began his career in 1578, but his most important contributions to the history of liberty came between 1606 and his death in 1634.

Coke's decisions as a judge often angered the king, but Coke never backed down. He opposed King James I's demands for more and more money to pay for his rich lifestyle. He also opposed James's attempts to influence court cases. In 1616, King James I fired Coke from his position for a time. Later, Coke had similar conflicts with Charles I, who became king in 1625.

In one of Coke's most famous decisions, he ruled common law was above Parliamentary statutes. He declared judges had the power to pronounce a law void, or invalid. Coke's **Petition** of Right, presented to Charles I in 1628, once again rejected the idea that monarchs are above the law. It declared

Edward Coke's Petition of Right claimed liberties for all people based on precedents, including the Magna Carta.

20

> **Fast Fact**
> The Petition of Right complained that the king had broken the Magna Carta's promise that no man could be arrested, imprisoned, stripped of his land or liberty, or sentenced to death except "by the lawful judgment of his peers, or by the law of the land."

some of Charles's acts illegal and demanded he honor common law. Importantly, Coke believed any failure to apply laws equally to all men was against the laws and customs of England. Equal rights for all would soon be a rallying cry for young democracies.

DEFENDING ONE'S CASTLE

In one famous case, Edward Coke wrote that a man's home is his castle and he has the right to defend it. That meant that royal sheriffs couldn't search a person's home for no reason, and people couldn't be forced to quarter, or house, soldiers. These ideas influenced many later generations, including the Founding Fathers of the United States. American revolutionaries such as Thomas Jefferson, John Adams, Patrick Henry, and James Madison admired Coke's ideas—and they acquired their understanding of the Magna Carta from Coke's writings. The idea of banning the quartering of soldiers was important to the American colonists, because England had forced colonists to house soldiers after the French and Indian War (1754–1763).

In 1775, Paul Revere engraved a state seal for Massachusetts that showed a soldier with a sword in one hand and the Magna Carta in the other.

INSPIRING A NEW NATION

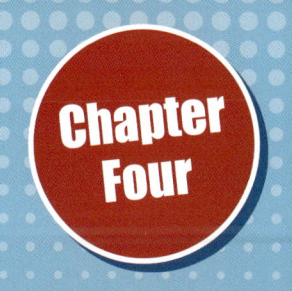

Chapter Four

The American colonies announced their separation from England in 1776. Their founding documents used ideas from the Magna Carta and Coke's writings on it. The words inspired a new nation that later inspired democracies around the world.

Declaration of Rights

In May 1776, at the request of the Virginia Convention, George Mason wrote a document called the Virginia Declaration of Rights. The document was brief, containing only 16 short sections. Among those sections were several that clearly shared the spirit of both the Magna Carta and Coke's writings. Like the

George Mason (1725–1792) embedded the ideals of the Magna Carta into the Virginia Declaration of Rights. The Virginia Convention approved the Declaration of Rights on June 12, 1776, making the spirit of the Magna Carta and Edward Coke part of the United States.

earlier documents, Mason's writing proclaimed there were limits on the government's power and the people possessed rights that couldn't be taken away. The Declaration of Rights proclaimed that power comes from the people and the rulers are their servants. It assured freedom from unreasonable searches and seizures and a speedy, fair trial for those accused of crimes. The document inspired other documents of the new nation, such as the Declaration of Independence and the U.S. Constitution.

> **Fast Fact**
>
> Thomas Jefferson once wrote that when he was studying law, all law students read Coke's writings. Jefferson praised Coke's understanding of English liberties in a letter to James Madison.

The Declaration of Independence

Thomas Jefferson was the author behind the Declaration of Independence, which formally announced the American colonies' separation from England in July 1776. We know how important Coke—and through him, the Magna Carta—was to Jefferson because of Jefferson's letters.

The task of drafting the Declaration of Independence fell on the Committee of Five—Thomas Jefferson, Benjamin Franklin, John Adams, Robert Livingston, and Roger Sherman.

Like the Magna Carta, the Declaration of Independence lists grievances against the king and points out ways he had ignored laws and mistreated his subjects. Also, influenced by Coke's ideas, the Declaration of Independence proclaims rights belong to all men, not just a chosen few. The Declaration also lists abuses of royal power such as the forced quartering of soldiers, taxation without the people's consent, and denying people trial by jury. It states that the power of government comes from the people.

Securing Rights and Liberties

In May 1787, state delegates to the what's now known as the Constitutional Convention met in Philadelphia, Pennsylvania, to improve the Articles of Confederation. This first constitution of the United States was in effect from 1781 to 1789, but it was beyond fixing. Delegates needed to make a whole new constitution—one that gave the central government enough power but also ensured the rights and liberties of the people.

George Washington presided over, or led, the Constitutional Convention. He would become the first president of the United States, an executive position limited in power by the U.S. Constitution.

James Madison is called the "Father of the Constitution" for his participation in writing and defending the U.S. Constitution.

The U.S. Constitution went into effect in 1789 and is still our governing document today. It sets up the framework for the U.S. government. It also includes room for further amendments as the country changes.

The Constitution reflects many ideas from the Magna Carta and Edward Coke's writings. Among the reasons for the Constitution listed in its preamble are to "establish Justice … and secure the Blessings of Liberty." The Constitution creates a government whose legislative, executive, and judicial branches have specific powers and also exercise power over each other. This system of checks and balances is designed to limit the government's power.

The barons who crafted the Magna Carta couldn't have imagined the impact they'd have on the future democracies of the world. They only wanted to reclaim rights from a tyrannical king. The Magna Carta may be more than 800 years old, but its principles established a precedent for equal rights and liberties for all.

Fast Fact
The Articles of Confederation purposefully created a weak central government, as a reaction to years of unfair treatment under the English monarchy. However, it made the government too weak to function effectively.

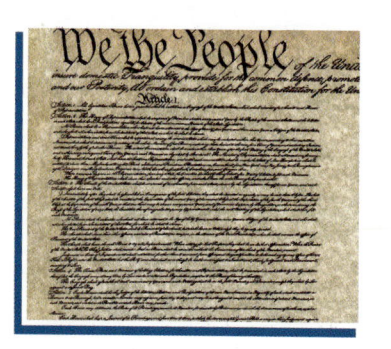

This copy of the Constitution shows the large letters of "We the People," which begins the preamble. Those three words declare that the power of the Constitution comes from the people.

THE BILL OF RIGHTS

The first 10 amendments to the U.S. Constitution are the Bill of Rights. They were added when some leaders complained loudly that the Constitution lacked any declaration of rights. They felt the door was open for the government to abuse its power without such a declaration. James Madison wrote the amendments, and, after approval by the states, the Bill of Rights was added. The First Amendment ensures the right to free speech and press and a right to protest and petition an unjust government. The Third Amendment keeps the government from forcing citizens to quarter soldiers. The Fourth amendment protects citizens from unreasonable search and seizure—important concerns in the Magna Carta.

Fast Fact

The founding documents of the United States also impacted the constitutions of other democratic governments, from France to Australia to Nigeria.

The Bill of Rights, shown here, ensures basic rights and liberties for all citizens of the United States.

HOW THE MAGNA CARTA INSPIRED DOCUMENTS OF DEMOCRACY

Declaration of Independence

- lists abuses of royal power
- proclaims rights belong to all men, not just a chosen few
- states power comes from the people

U.S. Constitution

- sets up a government in which no branch becomes too powerful
- states all citizens have rights, not just a few
- promises due process of law for those accused of crimes

Virginia Declaration of Rights

- ensures limits on government's power
- states people possess rights that can't be taken away and power comes from the people
- proclaims freedom from unreasonable searches and seizures
- allows for speedy, fair trials

THINK ABOUT IT!

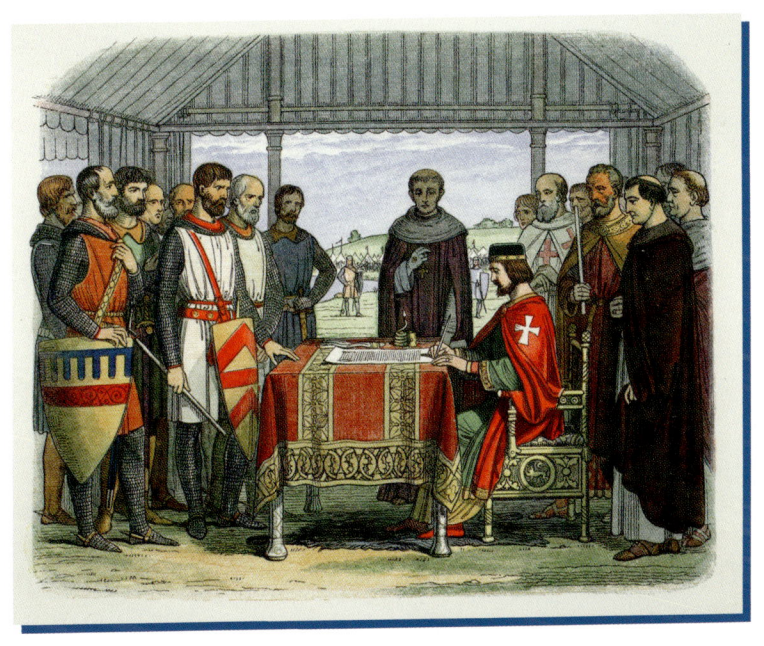

1. Why was the Magna Carta necessary?

2. How was the Magna Carta revolutionary in its ideas?

3. Why was it important for English kings to keep issuing and living by the Magna Carta?

4. What are some similarities between the concerns of the barons under King John in 1215 and the American colonists of the 18th century?

GLOSSARY

assail: To attack.

banish: To drive someone out of a place.

corruption: Dishonest or illegal behavior, especially by powerful people.

credible: Reliable or believable.

crusade: Any of the military missions led by the Catholic Church in the 11th to 13th centuries to spread the religion and regain the Holy Land.

democracy: The free and equal right of every person to participate in a government. Also, a government built on this principle.

deprive: To take something away from.

monarchy: A government headed by a king or queen.

Parliament: The British lawmaking body.

petition: A formal written request to a leader or government regarding a particular cause. Also, to make such a request.

precedent: Something done or said in the past that sets a model for the future.

statute: A law.

tyranny: Cruel and unfair treatment by people with power over others.

FIND OUT MORE

Books

Barrington, Richard. *The Magna Carta*. New York, NY: Britannica Educational Publishing, 2017.

Lüsted, Marcia Amidon. *The Magna Carta*. North Mankato, MN: Capstone Publishing, 2020.

Stuckey, Rachel. *Your Guide to Medieval Society*. St. Catharines, ON: Crabtree Publishing, 2017.

Websites

Magna Carta
www.dkfindout.com/us/more-find-out/what-does-politician-do/magna-carta/
Check out the Magna Carta with DK Find Out!

Middle Ages: King John and the Magna Carta
www.ducksters.com/history/middle_ages/king_john_magna_carta.php
Learn more about King John and the signing of the Magna Carta.

Project Britain: Magna Carta
www.projectbritain.com/calendar/June/magnacarta.html
Discover fun facts about the Magna Carta from Project Britain.

Publisher's note to educators and parents: Our editors have carefully reviewed these websites to ensure that they are suitable for students. Many websites change frequently, however, and we cannot guarantee that a site's future contents will continue to meet our high standards of quality and educational value. Be advised that students should be closely supervised whenever they access the Internet.

INDEX

A
Adams, John, 21, 24
Articles of the Barons, 8, 9
Articles of Confederation, 25, 26

B
Bill of Rights, 27

C
Charles I, King, 20
Charter of King John, 13
clause 13, 11
clause 33, 12
clause 35, 12
clause 39, 13
clause 40, 13
clause 61, 15
Coke, Edward, 19, 20, 21, 23, 24, 25, 26
common law, 19, 20
Constitution, U.S., 24, 25, 26, 27
Constitutional Convention, 25
Crusade, Third, 7

D
Declaration of Independence, 24, 25
due process, 13

E
Edward I, King, 17, 18
Elizabeth I, Queen, 19

F
Franklin, Benjamin, 24
French and Indian War, 21

H
Henry II, King, 4, 6
Henry III, King, 16, 17
Henry, Patrick, 21

J
James I, King, 20
Jefferson, Thomas, 21, 24
John (Lackland), King, 4, 6, 7, 8, 9, 10, 11, 13, 14, 17

L
Livingston, Robert, 24
London, England, 11, 13

M
Madison, James, 21, 24, 26, 27
Mason, George, 23, 24

P
Petition of Right, 20, 21

R
Richard I, King, 4, 6, 7
Robin Hood, 9

S
Sherman, Roger, 24

V
Virginia Declaration of Rights, 23, 24

W
Washington, George, 25